Nutrition

Proteins

by Brienna Rossiter

FOCUS READERS
BEACON

www.focusreaders.com

Focus Readers is distributed by North Star Editions:
sales@northstareditions.com | 888-417-0195

Produced for Focus Readers by Red Line Editorial.

Photographs ©: Shutterstock Images, cover, 1, 4, 6, 8, 10, 13, 14–15, 22, 25, 26; iStockphoto, 16, 19, 20, 29

Library of Congress Cataloging-in-Publication Data
Names: Rossiter, Brienna, author.
Title: Proteins / by Brienna Rossiter.
Description: Mendota Heights, MN: Focus Readers, [2025] | Series: Nutrition | Includes bibliographical references and index. | Audience: Grades 2-3
Identifiers: LCCN 2023053154 (print) | LCCN 2023053155 (ebook) | ISBN 9798889981848 (hardcover) | ISBN 9798889982401 (paperback) | ISBN 9798889983507 (pdf) | ISBN 9798889982968 (ebook)
Subjects: LCSH: Proteins in human nutrition--Juvenile literature. | Nutrition--Juvenile literature.
Classification: LCC QP551 .R843 2025 (print) | LCC QP551 (ebook) | DDC 572/.6--dc23/eng/20231229
LC record available at https://lccn.loc.gov/2023053154
LC ebook record available at https://lccn.loc.gov/2023053155

Printed in the United States of America
Mankato, MN
082024

About the Author

Brienna Rossiter is a writer and editor who lives in Minnesota.

Table of Contents

CHAPTER 1

Protein-Packed 5

CHAPTER 2

Building Blocks 9

Amino Acids 14

CHAPTER 3

Lots of Options 17

CHAPTER 4

Picking Proteins 23

Focus on Proteins • 28

Glossary • 30

To Learn More • 31

Index • 32

Chapter 1

Protein-Packed

A girl and her dad cook dinner together. For their main dish, they make curry. First, the girl's dad cuts chicken into small pieces. Then, he cooks it in a pan.

Curry is a sauce from India. It can be used with many types of proteins.

When cooking at home, people can control how much protein they eat.

Next, he cooks peppers and carrots. The girl mixes them with the chicken. She also adds a sauce. She adds a can of chickpeas, too. Chickpeas add even more protein to the dish.

The girl's dad makes rice. They pour the sauce, chicken, and chickpeas over it. They also eat a salad. They sprinkle sunflower seeds on top. The girl adds some shredded cheese as well. Their tasty meal contains many types of protein.

Did You Know?

When people think of eating protein, they often think of meat. But many plants can be good sources of protein, too.

Chapter 2

Building Blocks

Proteins are important **nutrients**. They are in every body part. Bones and muscles are made with proteins. So are skin and hair. Proteins are in blood, too.

Human bodies use thousands of different proteins.

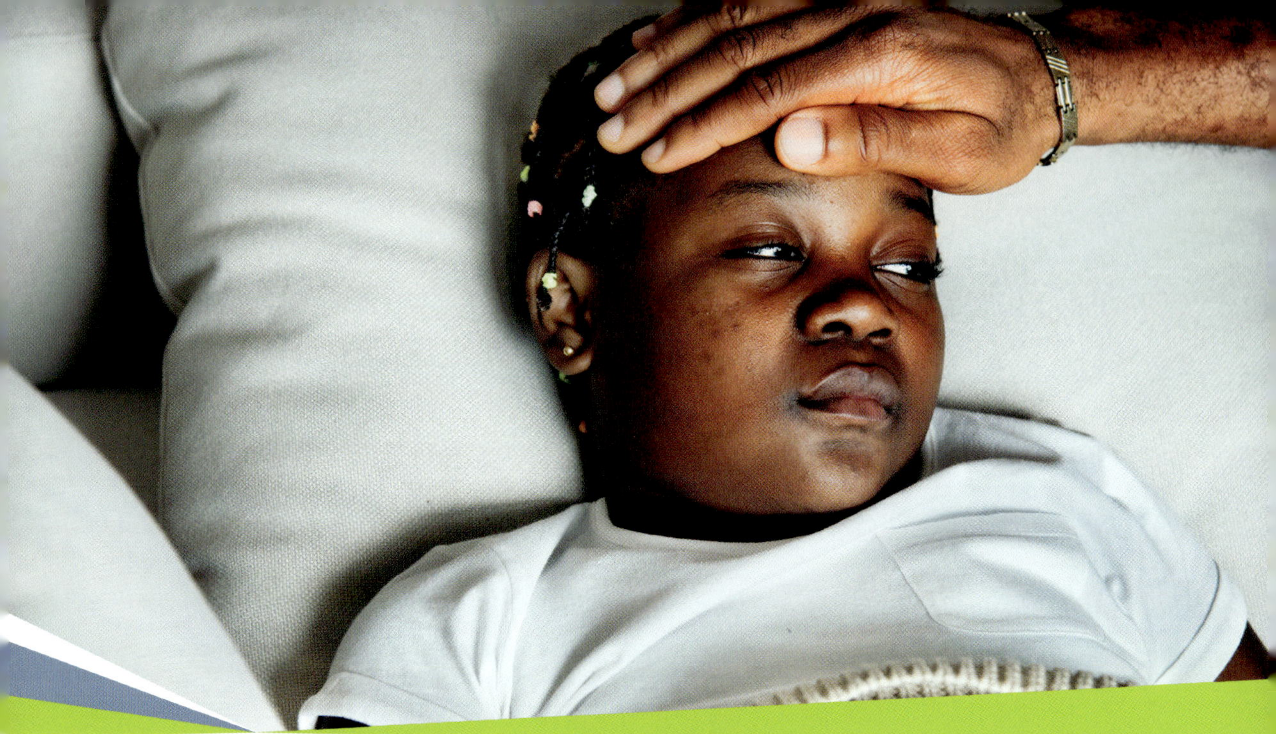

Without enough protein, people may feel weak. They can get sick more often.

The body needs proteins to form and repair **tissues**. This is especially true for kids. They are still growing.

Proteins allow the body to do many things. For example, they help make hormones. Hormones send **signals**. They help the body do certain tasks. Some hormones help the body get energy from food. Others can help when people get sick.

All proteins are made up of amino acids. Amino acids are like tiny building blocks. They link together to form chains. These chains can be long and complex. One protein may be made of thousands of amino acids.

Every protein is made of a unique set of amino acids. The amino acids go in a certain order. That order causes proteins to have different shapes. Differently shaped proteins do different things in the body. Some help grow tissues. Others act as messengers.

Different people need different amounts of protein. It depends on their age and size. It also depends on how active they are.

Most children ages 9 to 13 need about 34 grams of protein every day.

When people eat proteins, the body splits apart the amino acids. Then, the amino acids can be linked together in new ways. The body can create different proteins. Or it may use the amino acids for energy.

A CLOSER LOOK

Amino Acids

Amino acids can be sorted into different groups. Nine amino acids are essential. The body cannot make them on its own. To get them, people must eat certain foods. The other 11 amino acids are nonessential. The body still needs these types. However, it can make them from other foods or proteins.

When choosing foods, people should try to get all nine essential amino acids. Otherwise, their bodies won't be able to form some of the proteins they need.

Some amino acids are essential only when a person is sick or pregnant.

Chapter 3

Lots of Options

Proteins are in many foods. These foods are usually sorted into two groups. The first group comes from animals. Red meats are in this group. These meats include beef and pork.

Meats tend to have more protein per serving than other kinds of food.

Other kinds of meat have protein, too. They include fish and chicken. Eggs are another source of animal protein. So are dairy products. For example, milk has lots of protein. Yogurt and cheese do as well.

The second group of proteins comes from plants. Beans and peas are common sources. For instance, many people get proteins from chickpeas. People also get proteins from foods made out of soybeans.

Tempeh (left) and tofu (right) are examples of plant-based proteins made from soybeans.

Proteins are also found in nuts and seeds. Good sources include sunflower seeds and almonds. Certain vegetables and grains have small amounts of protein, too.

Chia seeds (left) and quinoa (right) are both nearly complete plant-based proteins.

Some of these sources are complete proteins. That means they contain all nine essential amino acids. Others are incomplete. They have smaller amounts of some amino acids. So, people must combine different foods. For instance, black beans and rice are a common mixture. When eaten together, these foods supply large amounts of all the essential amino acids.

Did You Know?

Most plant-based proteins are incomplete. But people can combine foods. That way, they can get all the proteins they need from a plant-based diet.

Chapter 4

Picking Proteins

Choosing good protein sources is important. Many foods have protein. But they contain other things, too. Some of these things are more helpful than others.

Eating different kinds of high-protein foods is a key part of a good diet.

For example, red meats contain all nine essential amino acids. However, they also have saturated fat. Eating too much of this fat can increase the risk of heart disease. So, experts suggest that people don't eat a lot of red meat.

Many dairy foods also have high levels of saturated fats. So, dairy foods are most helpful in small amounts. Chicken and seafood are healthier animal proteins. These foods have fewer harmful fats.

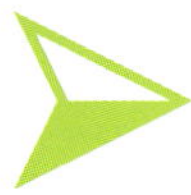

Baking, grilling, and steaming are healthy ways to cook protein.

Experts say people should avoid **processed** protein sources. These foods include hot dogs and lunch meat. Bacon and sausage are also examples of processed proteins.

Eating plant-based foods can decrease risks of some diseases.

Processed meats contain large amounts of salt and fat. They also contain **preservatives**. Eating lots of these foods is bad for the body.

Experts suggest choosing more plant-based foods. These foods can have lots of protein. They have other nutrients, too. For example, beans are high in **fiber**.

Producing animal-based foods uses huge amounts of energy and water. It also releases **greenhouse gases**. These gases make **climate change** worse. Most plant-based foods use far less energy and water.

Some companies make protein powder. It can be helpful for athletes or older people. However, most people get enough protein from foods.

FOCUS ON
Proteins

Write your answers on a separate piece of paper.

1. Write a sentence describing one way the body uses proteins.
2. What is your favorite source of protein? What do you like about it?
3. Which word describes amino acids that people must get by eating certain foods?
   A. essential
   B. nonessential
   C. incomplete
4. Why would proteins be especially important for kids who are still growing?
   A. Their bodies use less energy than adults' bodies.
   B. Their bodies need more types of amino acids.
   C. Their bodies must form new tissues to keep growing.

5. What does **complex** mean in this book?

*These chains can be long and **complex**. One protein may be made of thousands of amino acids.*

A. having old parts or pieces
B. having few parts or pieces
C. having many parts or pieces

6. What does **unique** mean in this book?

*Every protein is made of a **unique** set of amino acids. The amino acids go in a certain order. That order causes proteins to have different shapes.*

A. the same as all others
B. not like others
C. unable to mix together

Answer key on page 32.

Glossary

athletes
People who play sports.

climate change
A human-caused global crisis involving long-term changes in Earth's temperature and weather patterns.

fiber
The tough parts of plants that are hard for the body to break down.

greenhouse gases
Gases that trap heat in Earth's atmosphere, causing climate change.

nutrients
Substances that living things need to stay strong and healthy.

preservatives
Chemicals that are added to food to make it last longer.

processed
When food is changed by adding something to it or preparing it in a certain way.

signals
Ways of sending information.

tissues
Groups of similar cells in a plant or animal that have certain functions.

To Learn More

BOOKS

Nissenberg, Sandra K. *The Everything Kids' Cookbook: 90+ Easy Recipes You'll Love to Make and Eat!* New York: Adams Media, 2020.

Rea, Amy C. *Proteins as Necessary Nutrients*. Minneapolis: Abdo Publishing, 2023.

Rebman, Nick. *Earth-Friendly Eating*. Mendota Heights, MN: Focus Readers, 2022.

NOTE TO EDUCATORS

Visit **www.focusreaders.com** to find lesson plans, activities, links, and other resources related to this title.

Index

A

amino acids, 11–13, 14, 20–21, 24

B

bones, 9

C

climate change, 27
curry, 5

D

dairy, 18, 24

F

fiber, 27

G

greenhouse gases, 27

H

hormones, 11

M

muscles, 9

P

preservatives, 26
processed, 25–26

R

red meats, 17, 24

S

saturated fat, 24

T

tissues, 10, 12

Answer Key: 1. Answers will vary; **2.** Answers will vary; **3.** A; **4.** C; **5.** C; **6.** B